DATE DUE

DEMCO 38-296

Unlimited, Unexplored, and Unexplained

Scientific Advancements of the 19th Century

Guglielmo Marconi

and the Story of Radio Waves

Mitchell Lane
PUBLISHERS

P.O. Box 196
Hockessin, Delaware 19707

Uncharted, Unexplored, and Unexplained

Scientific Advancements of the 19th Century

Titles in the Series

Visit us on the web: www.mitchelllane.com
Comments? email us: mitchelllane@mitchelllane.com

Uncharted, Unexplored, and Unexplained

Scientific Advancements of the 19th Century

Guglielmo Marconi
and the Story of Radio Waves

by Susan Zannos

Uncharted, Unexplored, and Unexplained

Scientific Advancements of the 19th Century

Copyright © 2005 by Mitchell Lane Publishers, Inc. All rights reserved. No part of this book may be reproduced without written permission from the publisher. Printed and bound in the United States of America.

Printing   1   2   3   4   5   6   7   8

Library of Congress Cataloging-in-Publication Data

Zannos, Susan.

Guglielmo Marconi and radio waves / Susan Zannos.

p. cm. — (Uncharted, unexplored & unexplained, scientific advancements of the 19th century)

Includes bibliographical references and index.

Contents: The dinner plates—Moving around—Farther and farther—All the ships at sea—Businessman and politician.

ISBN 1-58415-265-6 (Library Bound)

1. Marconi, Guglielmo, marchese, 1874–1937—Juvenile literature. 2. Telegraph, Wireless—History—Juvenile literature. 3. Radio—History—Juvenile literature. 4. Radio waves—Juvenile literature. 5. Inventors—Italy—Biography—Juvenile literature. [1. Marconi, Guglielmo, marchese, 1874–1937. 2. Inventors. 3. Radio—History.] I. Title. II. Uncharted, unexplored, & unexplained

TK5739.M3Z35 2004

621.384'092—dc22

2003024133

ABOUT THE AUTHOR: Susan Zannos has been a lifelong educator, having taught at all levels, from preschool to college, in Mexico, Greece, Italy, Russia, and Lithuania, as well as in the United States. She has published a mystery *Trust the Liar* (Walker and Co.) and *Human Types: Essence and the Enneagram* (Samuel Weiser). Her book, *Human Types*, was recently translated into Russian, and in 2003 Susan was invited to tour Russia and lecture about her book. Another book she wrote for young adults, *Careers in Education* (Mitchell Lane) was selected for the New York Public Library's "Books for the Teen Age 2003 List." She has written many books for children, including *Chester Carlson and the Development of Xerography* and *The Life and Times of Ludwig van Beethoven* (Mitchell Lane). When not traveling, Susan lives in the Sierra Foothills of Northern California.

PHOTO CREDITS: Cover, pp. 1, 3, 9, 14, 34—Corbis; pp. 6, 9, 20, 22, 28, 31, 36—Getty Images/Hulton Archive; pp. 10, 11, 12, 16, 18, 39, 41—Marconi Collection; p. 19—Georgia State University; p. 35—University of Tennessee; p. 40—Michael Ritter.

PUBLISHER'S NOTE: This story is based on the author's extensive research, which she believes to be accurate. Documentation of such research is contained on page 47.

The internet sites referenced herein were active as of the publication date. Due to the fleeting nature of some web sites, we cannot guarantee they will all be active when you are reading this book.

Uncharted, Unexplored, and Unexplained

Scientific Advancements of the 19th Century

Guglielmo Marconi

and the Story of Radio Waves

*For Your Information

Guglielmo Marconi was only 22 years old when he traveled to England and patented his device for sending messages using electromagnetic waves. With financing from the British government, he demonstrated that he could communicate by wireless transmitters and receivers not only across land but across water as well.

1

The Dinner Plates

Villagers and visitors to the spa at Porretta, Italy, paused in their stroll across the bridge. They glanced down at the boy by the side of the stream. He had placed what appeared to be a set of dinner plates in a row in the water. The plates were held in place by strings. What was he doing? They couldn't figure it out.

The boy was Guglielmo Marconi. He had been reading about Benjamin Franklin. He was fascinated with Franklin's experiments with electricity. Now he was conducting his own experiments. He knew that water conducted electricity, and he had read that porcelain was not a conductor. Well, dinner plates were porcelain, weren't they? What would happen if electricity were sent through water and porcelain at the same time?

He soon found out. He sent a jolt of electricity through the strings. The shock sent the plates crashing onto the rocks at the bottom of the stream, breaking them all. The passers-by laughed and went on their way shaking their heads. The boy must be crazy.

There was one witness to the scene who was not smiling. It was Guglielmo's father. Giuseppe Marconi was very, very angry. He was a successful Italian landowner who managed his estate with thrift. If there was one thing Giuseppe could not tolerate, it was wastefulness.

This wasn't the first time that Giuseppe had objected to Guglielmo's experiments. The contraptions that the boy was forever fiddling with used expensive materials. One time the boy had taken his cousin Daisy's new sewing machine apart and made it into a roasting spit for meat. When Daisy burst into tears, Guglielmo put the sewing machine back together again so it stitched as well as before. Still, his father thought, he shouldn't have taken it apart in the first place.

Before the episode of the broken plates, Guglielmo's mother Annie had been able to defend the boy and calm his father down. Afterwards, however, her efforts were of no use. With the smashing of the dinner plates, his son had gone too far! Every time Giuseppe found one of Guglielmo's contraptions, he destroyed it. Mother and son became conspirators to hide the boy's experiments from his father.

The tensions in the family between father and son—both stubborn, and the two of them more alike than they would admit—may have been one reason that Annie traveled frequently, taking her children with her. The official reason was that her health was too delicate for the cold damp winters at Villa Griffone, the family estate in the countryside just outside of Bologna. They frequently spent the winter months in Florence in central Italy or at Leghorn on the west coast. Annie had English relatives in Leghorn that she liked to visit.

Guglielmo too liked visiting Leghorn, which is also known as Livorno. His favorite cousin, Daisy, lived there. But he preferred being at the Villa Griffone. It was easy to find the materials he needed for his experiments.

Guglielmo Marconi was fascinated by electricity. He read everything he could find about the experiments scientists were doing with this amazing phenomenon. Then he tried to do the experiments himself. By the time he was 20 years old, young Marconi was spending nearly all his time on his reading and his experiments.

He read about the theories of James Clerk Maxwell. Maxwell thought that changes in the amount of electricity in a wire would send out waves called electromagnetic waves, because they were composed of both

Left: Scottish scientist James Clerk Maxwell (1831–1879) developed the theory that changes in the amount of electricity in a wire would cause electromagnetic waves to spread out through the air. Right: In 1887 Heinrich Rudolph Hertz (1857–1894) showed that electromagnetic waves spread out from an induction coil and caused a spark to jump in a receiver several yards away.

magnetism and electricity. These waves, Maxwell believed, would spread out in the same way as ripples in a pond when a rock is dropped into the water. The waves would travel at the speed of light. In fact, light itself was one form of electromagnetic wave.

He also read about the experiments of Heinrich Hertz, who had proven Maxwell's theories. Hertz developed equipment that would send out and detect electromagnetic waves across a distance of several yards.

Guglielmo and his older brother Alfonso were vacationing in the Swiss Alps in 1894, the year that Hertz died. While trying to get to sleep in the hotel one night, Guglielmo suddenly had an idea. For nearly half a century, electrical signals had been used to send messages along telegraph wires. Why couldn't those messages be sent without wires by using the electromagnetic waves Hertz had discovered?

"Wireless telegraphy" was such an obvious idea, he thought. Surely others would have thought of it. But no one had. The fear that someone would gave urgency and direction to his experiments. Now Guglielmo thought of almost nothing else. Back at the Villa Griffone, he begged his mother to let him use the attic rooms for a laboratory. Somehow Annie managed to convince her husband. When the summer was over and it was time for the family to move away from Bologna to a milder climate, Guglielmo said he wouldn't go. His mother, even though she suffered from the cold, decided they would all stay at the villa.

The attic rooms had not been used since Guglielmo's grandfather had used them to breed silkworms. The trays he had used were still stored there. The young Marconi did not need much space. His materials were simple: copper wire, some zinc and copper sheets, glass tubes full of metal filings, and batteries.

The attic consisted of two rooms separated by an archway. At one end Guglielmo set up a transmitter that would reproduce the one Hertz had used. It consisted of two layers of wire wound around an iron core. The low-voltage electricity from a battery flowed through the first wire. When periodically interrupted, it induced a high-voltage in the second coil of wire. The high voltage produced a spark that jumped the gap between two electrodes. This discharge of electricity generated the electromagnetic waves that radiated out from the spark.

This device is the original coherer/receiver that Marconi built in his attic workroom to demonstrate that electromagnetic waves could be used to transmit an electrical impulse without using wires.

At the other end of the attic Guglielmo placed the detector. This was a glass tube called a coherer that contained metal filings. When the filings received an electrical impulse, they stuck together, or cohered, and conducted the electricity. In his first successful breakthrough, which happened in the middle of the night, the electromagnetic waves rang a tiny bell at the other end of his laboratory. Guglielmo was so excited that he went downstairs and woke up his mother so she could share his triumph. Shivering in the cold attic, Annie may not have understood what the ringing bell meant. She understood that her son had achieved something of great importance to him.

Guglielmo continued his experiments night and day. His father became more and more furious, blaming his mother for encouraging

Marconi continued to simplify his coherer/receivers to make them more sensitive to receiving messages over longer and longer distances. In addition, he made the transmitters more powerful so that they sent stronger electrical impulses.

him. His mother worried because he was losing weight and had dark circles under his eyes from lack of sleep. Young Marconi was driven by the fear that someone else would perfect the wireless system before he did.

"My chief trouble was that the idea was so elementary, so simple in logic that it seemed difficult to believe no one else had thought of putting it in practice," he said later. "The idea was so real to me that I did not realize that to others the theory might appear quite fantastic."[1]

Into this tense household—Guglielmo locked in the attic, Giuseppe stomping and complaining downstairs, and Annie sneaking dinner trays up to leave outside the attic door—Guglielmo's cousins suddenly arrived. Daisy and her three sisters came for a visit despite the stormy winter weather. Laughing and calling to him, the girls pounded on the attic door until Guglielmo finally gave up and opened it. Once inside the attic, the girls looked at the few pieces of mysterious equipment. It was rather disappointing, but Daisy asked him what he had found out with his experiments.

He took a compass and put it on the opposite side of the room, telling the girls he would make it move without touching it. Daisy wrote

This is the attic workroom Marconi used at Villa Griffone to conduct his experiments with electromagnetic waves. With very little money to buy equipment, he used what he could find on his father's estate and in his mother's kitchen to construct the transmitters and receivers he needed.

later, "Guglielmo then seated himself before an ordinary electric pear shaped glass from which a blue light played. He touched the small globe and in an instant both the needle and the compass began to move simultaneously."[2]

The girls suspected some trick. They thought perhaps a thread connected the two. They ran their fingers over and under the compass before they were convinced. They didn't know what they had seen, but they knew it was wonderful and mysterious. At lunch that day they talked excitedly about what they had seen while Giuseppe scowled and grumbled. Still, the excitement in the house did make the old farmer wonder what was going on in the attic.

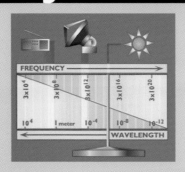

One of the most important scientific discoveries in the 19th century was the existence of electromagnetic waves. In research that began in 1864, a Scottish scientist named James Clerk Maxwell developed the theory that changes in the amount of electricity in a wire would send out waves through the air. These waves would spread out like the ripples in a pond when a rock is dropped into the water.

In 1887, German scientist Heinrich Hertz proved Maxwell's theory. Hertz made a transmitter from a coil of wire and an electricity supply with high voltage. It was broken by a space between two metal bars. When Hertz turned on the high voltage, a spark jumped between the two bars. When he put a spark-gap receiver a few yards away, a spark jumped there, too. This showed that electromagnetic waves had traveled from the transmitter to the receiver.

Electromagnetic waves are a form of energy that combines an electrical field with a magnetic field. They travel at the speed of light. They can travel through air, through liquids, and even through space. They can be measured in several ways: by their wavelength (the distance between the peaks of the waves), their frequency, and their energy.

The different wavelengths of electromagnetic waves are received as different kinds of energy. The longest waves, some of them many yards long, are radio waves. Next come microwaves, which can be between a third of a yard and less than an inch in length. Much shorter are infrared or heat waves. Then come light rays, the visible range of electromagnetic waves. Even shorter are ultraviolet rays, X rays, and Gamma rays.

Nearly all of the electronic technology developed during the past century is the result of using electromagnetic waves. Radio, television, microwave ovens, radar, cellular telephones, satellite communications, and many other inventions are all based on electromagnetic waves.

Guglielmo Marconi with his mother, Annie, and older brother, Alfonso. Marconi's mother was his strongest supporter, protecting him from his father, who believed the boy's experiments were foolishness. Alfonso assisted the young inventor with his early efforts at sending messages with electromagnetic waves.

2

Moving Around

Guglielmo Marconi was born on April 25, 1874. He was a child of two cultures. His mother, Annie Jameson, was the youngest daughter of a wealthy Irish landowner. She had a beautiful singing voice and had been invited to sing in London while she was still a teenager. Her family refused to allow it. To console Annie, they sent her to Bologna, Italy, to study music.

Annie stayed with friends of her parents in Bologna. Soon she met a handsome Italian widower, Giuseppe Marconi. Even though he was 17 years older than she was, the two fell in love. Her very conservative family was horrified when she returned home and told them she wanted to marry a foreigner. Annie Jameson did not make a fuss. She remained patiently in Ireland and secretly exchanged letters with Giuseppe. As soon as she turned 21, she left home and made her way to the city of Boulogne, France. Giuseppe traveled from Italy to meet her there. They were married the same day.

Annie and Giuseppe Marconi had their first son, Alfonso, a year after their romantic elopement. Nine years later their second son, Guglielmo was born. According to a family story, one old servant said of the baby, "What big ears he has!" His mother replied, "All the better to hear the still small voices of the air."[1]

By the time Guglielmo was born, the large differences in age and cultures between Annie and Giuseppe had produced differences in their lifestyles. Giuseppe stayed at the Villa Griffone, the family home in the country near Bologna. He enjoyed the life of a thrifty farm manager and took pride in his crops and harvests. Annie was still young and attractive. She liked having an active social life and she liked to travel. She normally left Villa Griffone for the winter months, on the pretext of being too frail to endure the harsh conditions. Her favorite destination was Leghorn, which not only had a milder climate but also an English colony that included Annie's older sister and four cousins for the Marconi boys to play with.

The Villa Griffone was the Marconi family estate in the northern Italian countryside. It was in the attic of the villa that Marconi conducted his first experiments with electromagnetism. Later he sent wireless messages across the garden, and still later across the fields while his brother Alfonso signaled when the messages were received.

Annie took her sons to England on several occasions. Their longest visit occurred when Guglielmo was three years old. They remained in England for three years, so he spoke English as his first language. All of this moving about prevented the boys from attending school regularly. When they returned to Italy she tutored them in English herself. For their other studies they had tutors, but Guglielmo was not an eager student.

Annie and the boys were in Florence the year that her younger son was 12. Giuseppe decided that Guglielmo should be enrolled in a regular school. The boy was miserable there. The other boys teased and tormented him because he spoke Italian with an English accent. The teachers were not much better. He was far behind his age group in his studies and his teachers ridiculed his poor work. One day the principal came to the classroom. He told Guglielmo, "Your Italian is atrocious. Now recite the Manzioni poem you have been studying. And speak up!"[2]

When Guglielmo tried to recite the poem, the other boys broke into loud laughter. They imitated his accent. But the teasing of the others did not shake Guglielmo's sense of his own worth. Years later he wrote, "I would try to hide from everybody—in order not to be teased—my irresistible feeling that one day I would be able to do something new and great. . . . They will realize one day—I used to say to myself—that I am not as dumb as they think."[3]

The only positive result of that year of suffering was the one friend he made: Luigi Solari. Their friendship would last for life, and Solari would assist him in many ways throughout his career.

The next year the family moved to Leghorn. It was much more to Guglielmo's liking. For one thing his favorite cousin, Daisy, lived there. But the main attraction was the sea. All of his life Guglielmo loved ships and the sea. He wanted to attend the naval academy at Leghorn—and for once he and his father agreed. Giuseppe liked the idea of his son becoming a naval officer. He even bought the boy a sailboat.

Unfortunately, the boy's expertise at sailing was not equaled by success with his studies. He failed to qualify for entrance to the naval academy. His father was bitterly disappointed. He thought that Guglielmo was wasting his time with useless activities instead of preparing himself for a respectable career.

In Leghorn, Guglielmo was sent to a private technical school, the Istituto Nazionale. There, for the first time, the boy found classes that interested him. His physics tutor taught him things that he could then use in his private experiments. When his mother realized his enthusiasm for science, she found the best electro physics instructor in Leghorn to give her son private lessons.

It was this man, Vincenzo Rosa, who was able to teach the boy the current theories about electricity and electromagnetic waves. For the rest of his life Guglielmo gave Professor Rosa credit for providing the "clear and practical method which started me in the study of electrophysics."[4]

Guglielmo met another man that year who provided a practical skill that would serve him well. Nello Marchetti was an old man who had been a telegraph operator. Now he was going blind. Guglielmo liked Marchetti and often went to his house to read to him. In spite of the difference in their ages they became good friends. Marchetti taught his young friend Morse code, the series of dots and dashes that were used in sending telegraph messages.

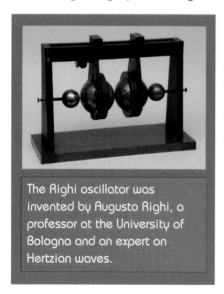

The Righi oscillator was invented by Augusto Righi, a professor at the University of Bologna and an expert on Hertzian waves.

When the Marconi family returned to the Villa Griffone the next year, Guglielmo again disappointed his father. He was unable to pass the examination that would allow him to attend the University of Bologna. Once again, his mother came to his rescue. A well known professor of physics, Augusto Righi, had a country home near the Villa Griffone. Annie spoke with Professor Righi and arranged for Guglielmo to use the library and the laboratory at the university even though he was not a student.

Although Righi was an accepted authority in the study of electromagnetic waves, he was not much interested when young Marconi first thought of using them to send messages. In fact, the professor thought the idea was ridiculous. Guglielmo, who had just begun his experiments in the attic of Villa Griffone, was afraid that someone would discover a way to use his idea before he could. He would ask the professor questions, but did not tell him about his secret experiments. Those experiments, sometimes started in the laboratory at the university but completed behind locked doors in the attic at Villa Griffone, would soon produce results that Professor Righi and other professional scientists believed were impossible.

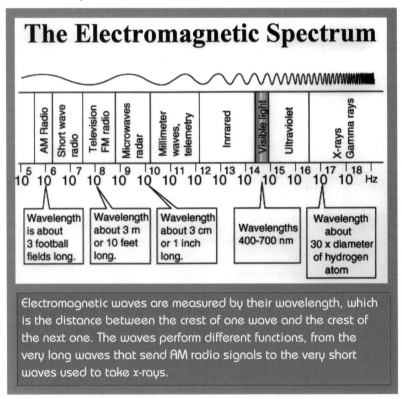

The Electromagnetic Spectrum

| AM Radio | Short wave radio | Television FM radio | Microwaves radar | Millimeter waves, telemetry | Inrrared | Visible light | Ultraviolet | X-rays | Gamma rays |

10^5 10^6 10^7 10^8 10^9 10^{10} 10^{11} 10^{12} 10^{13} 10^{14} 10^{15} 10^{16} 10^{17} 10^{18} Hz

| Wavelength is about 3 football fields long. | Wavelength about 3 m or 10 feet long. | Wavelength about 3 cm or 1 inch long. | Wavelengths 400-700 nm | Wavelength about 30 x diameter of hydrogen atom |

Electromagnetic waves are measured by their wavelength, which is the distance between the crest of one wave and the crest of the next one. The waves perform different functions, from the very long waves that send AM radio signals to the very short waves used to take x-rays.

In later years when reporters asked Marconi if he had studied with Righi, he said, "I studied under the renowned Professor Vincenzo Rosa at the Livorno Lyceum and would be most happy that it be known that he was my only physics master."[5]

For his part, Professor Righi never claimed to have been Marconi's teacher. When reporters asked him if he had been, he replied, "I should be very happy to deserve such a title, but it would be necessary to give the word a wide meaning to apply it to someone who had only a few conversations with the young inventor."[6]

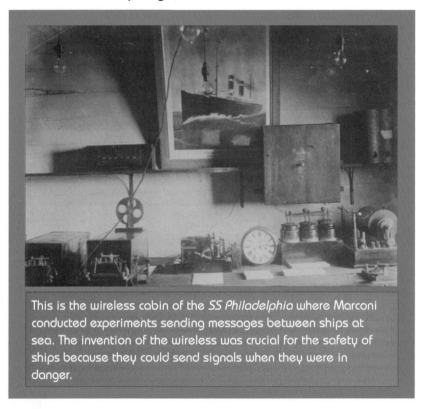

This is the wireless cabin of the *SS Philadelphia* where Marconi conducted experiments sending messages between ships at sea. The invention of the wireless was crucial for the safety of ships because they could send signals when they were in danger.

Righi made the difference between a scientist and an inventor very clear. A scientist is someone whose experiments reveal the fundamental laws of nature. An inventor is someone who uses those laws for practical purposes. Righi the scientist and Marconi the inventor were involved in basically different activities. Righi studied the nature of electromagnetic waves. Marconi was only interested in using the waves to communicate over long distances. The young man had little interest in what the mysterious waves were. His concern was with what they could do. He devoted his life to sending messages over longer and longer distances.

Samuel Morse, born in 1791, was a professional artist. In 1832 he was returning to America after living and painting in Europe for several years. During the voyage he heard a conversation about electromagnets. From this he had the idea of sending messages through electric wires.

Morse was not a scientist or an inventor, but he soon demonstrated the ability of a telegraph system to transmit information over wires. From 1837 on he gave all his attention to developing the telegraph (the word comes from Greek words meaning "distance writing"). In 1844 Morse demonstrated to Congress that the telegraph was practical. He sent the message "What hath God wrought" from Washington, D.C., to Baltimore, Maryland.

Before the invention of Morse's telegraph, messages could take days, weeks or even months to arrive at their destination. On land, most messages could travel no faster than the fastest horse. Messages between America to Europe had to go by ship.

The telegraph was the first invention that used electricity to send messages. An operator tapped a telegraph key. This key controlled the flow of electricity along a wire. At the other end of the wire a receiver changed the electrical impulses to dots and dashes on a paper tape. Morse devised a code that used these dots and dashes to represent the letters of the alphabet.

Morse code uses units of time. A dot uses one unit and a dash three units, with three units pause between letters and seven units pause between words. An experienced telegraph operator could send or receive 20 to 30 words per minute.

INTERNATIONAL MORSE CODE

A ● —	N — ●	1 ● — — — —	Ñ — — ● — —	N with tilde
B — ● ● ●	O — — —	2 ● ● — — —	Ö — — — ●	O with umlaut
C — ● — ●	P ● — — ●	3 ● ● ● — —	Ü ● ● — —	U with umlaut
D — ● ●	Q — — ● —	4 ● ● ● ● —	, ● ● — ● ●	comma
E ●	R ● — ●	5 ● ● ● ● ●	. ● — ● — ● —	period
F ● ● — ●	S ● ● ●	6 — ● ● ● ●	? ● ● — — ● ●	question mark
G — — ●	T —	7 — — ● ● ●	; — ● — ● — ●	semicolon
H ● ● ● ●	U ● ● —	8 — — — ● ●	: — — — ● ● ●	colon
I ● ●	V ● ● ● —	9 — — — — ●	/ — ● ● — ●	slash
J ● — — —	W ● — —	0 — — — — —	- — ● ● ● ● —	dash
K — ● —	X — ● ● —	Á ● — — ● —	A with accent	' ● — — — — ●	apostrophe
L ● — ● ●	Y — ● — —	Ä ● — ● —	A with umlaut	() — ● — — ● —	parenthesis
M — —	Z — — ● ●	É ● ● — ● ●	E with accent	_ ● ● — — ● —	underline

Guglielmo Marconi and English technician George Kemp, at work in their laboratory. Kemp became Marconi's first assistant when the English government began financing his experiments. The two men worked together until the end of Marconi's life.

Scientific Advancements of the 19th Century

3

Farther and Farther

Guglielmo Marconi could go no farther in the attic. He'd sent and received electromagnetic waves the distance of the two attic rooms—and even from the attic to other rooms in the house. He'd carried his experiments as far as he could with the equipment he'd been able to buy with the small amounts of money his mother was able to give him. It was time for him to come out of the attic. It was time for him to face his father.

Giuseppe Marconi listened as his son described his experiments in detail and spoke of the possibility of wireless communications. For the first time, Guglielmo felt that his father was really listening and taking him seriously. When he demonstrated his process by ringing a bell, Giuseppe wanted more proof. The young inventor changed the sending apparatus to a telegraph tapper and sent the three dots for the letter S in Morse code. This signal was to become the one he used in all his experiments.

It was clear that his father was impressed. But when Guglielmo asked for money, his father demanded that he explain the possibilities of future developments. Annie pleaded with her husband to provide money on faith alone. The old farm manager was too business-like for that. He explained that his son would have to have financing from banks and businessmen who would not provide it on faith.

Guglielmo was crushed, feeling that he had failed. As he turned away, his father reached into his pocket and took out 500 lira. It was more than the young man had asked for, and more than enough for the equipment he needed. He had achieved two victories. He had the money to continue. Much more important, from that day on he had the respect and advice of the father who had opposed him ever since he began his experiments.

Encouraged by knowing that his entire family was now behind him, Guglielmo worked even harder. He moved out into the garden. He replaced the two balls of the oscillator (the device across which the spark jumped) with two metal sheets that he took from an old gas tank. He linked one of these sheets to the earth while he lifted the other into the air. In a letter to his friend Luigi Solari he explained, "I then discovered the way to transmit waves at distances of hundreds of meters. By chance I set one of the iron sheets at a considerable distance from the ground and the other on the earth. Thanks to this position, the signals become so strong that I could extend the transmission range to a kilometer [about five-eighths of a mile]. I saw then for the first time a great new way opened to me."[1]

What Marconi said was "chance" was actually the result of long hours and days and weeks of careful experiments. Even though the accepted scientific opinion was that electromagnetic waves could not radiate far enough for practical use, Marconi believed that they could. Hertz had believed that the waves obeyed the same laws as light waves. If that was so, then it should be possible to extend the distance they traveled by increasing the power of the sending apparatus and the sensitivity of the receiver. Marconi said, "If we had attributed to the power of light only the possibilities offered by a candle, we would never have built lighthouses and reflectors."[2]

In experiment after experiment he increased the distance he could send the signals. His brother Alfonso stood in the garden by the receiver while Guglielmo operated the transmitter and watched from his laboratory window. He tapped out the three dots. Alfonso checked the reception of the signal and waved a handkerchief on a pole so his brother could see when the signal was successfully received: 100 meters, then 200, 400, and even 600 meters away.

Finally, one late summer morning in 1895, Alfonso set off with two assistants who helped carry the antennas and receiving equipment. They walked for 20 minutes, passing the farm buildings near the house and disappearing over the top of a hill. Alfonso was carrying a rifle. They were going too far for Guglielmo to be able to see the handkerchief. He waited for several minutes. Then he began sending the three dots with the Morse key. In the still morning air a shot rang out. The signal had been received over a mile away!

That rifle shot made it clear that it was time to move on. It was time to present Guglielmo's invention to the world. But how? The family talked the matter over with respected members of the community. After much discussion, the Marconis wrote a letter to the Italian Minister of Post and Telegraph. They thought he would be the person most interested in a new method of communication.

A minor clerk answered with a letter that gave them little encouragement but said perhaps the invention would be of use for ships. The Marconis' were angered by Italy's lack of interest. Annie, always the first to rush in with help for her youngest son, decided they should go to England. After all, England had the most powerful shipping interests in the world.

Among Annie's many English relatives was a nephew, Henry Jameson-Davis. He had a degree in engineering and many contacts in the scientific world. Henry met Annie and Guglielmo at the train station when they arrived in London and immediately began to assist them. The first step, they all agreed, was to get a patent for Guglielmo's invention. They did so. The second step was to find someone in the British government who would sponsor further experiments.

Henry Jameson-Davis's efforts led to Marconi's introduction to Sir William Preece, the chief engineer of the English Post and Telegraph Services. The day that the two met in the spring of 1896 was one of the most important moments in Guglielmo Marconi's life. Preece had himself done experiments in sending and receiving Hertz waves, so he knew exactly what the young Italian had accomplished.

Guglielmo conducted many experiments for Sir William, and the two became good friends. One of Preece's best technicians, George Kemp, became Marconi's first assistant. Kemp would remain with Marconi until the end of his life. The young Italian's ability to inspire others who worked with him was almost as important in the success of his efforts as his single-minded determination.

By the time of his demonstrations for Preece, Guglielmo had already connected a Morse code recorder to his receiving circuit. He had found this important piece of equipment in a junk shop in Bologna and bought it with part of the money his father had given him. In one of the first open-air demonstrations, Marconi and Preece transmitted signals from the roof of the Post Office to the roof of another building a mile away. There were several tall buildings in between. After this success Preece told Guglielmo to do long range experiments in the country.

With the British government financing his experiments, Marconi set eagerly to work. By now the army and navy as well as the Post Office department were interested. The press published accounts of the young Italian inventor's work. Not everyone was enthusiastic. Some of the worst attacks came from the scientists who still believed that using electromagnetic waves for communication was impossible. Lord Kelvin, one of the most respected scientists in England, said, "Wireless is all very well, but I would rather send a message by a boy on a pony."[3]

Although Marconi was by then only 22 years old, the interviews he gave to the newspaper reporters show the maturity and caution, as well as the business sense, of a far older man. He was not only a brilliant inventor. He was also clearly Giuseppe Marconi's son.

Transatlantic Cable

Before the invention of the telegraph, the only way to send messages between Europe and America was by ship. As a result, news took weeks to arrive. For example, the Treaty of Ghent was signed on December 24, 1814. It ended the War of 1812 between England and the United States. But the most decisive battle of the war, the Battle of New Orleans, was fought on January 8, 1815 because no one knew the war was over. More than 2,000 men died needlessly.

Soon after the first telegraph message was sent between Washington and Baltimore in 1844, people began to think about connecting the North American continent to Europe with cable that could carry messages. But the long distance and the depth of the sea were big obstacles.

In August, 1857, two ships loaded with cable, the American Niagara and the British Agamemnon, left Valentia Harbor in Ireland to lay the cable. Six days later the cable snapped when the brakes that slowed the descent suddenly jammed. Only 380 miles of cable had been laid. The ships had to return to port.

Machinery used for paying out the electric telegraph on board the *Agamemnon* and *Niagara*.

They tried again the following year. After several failures, both ships reached their ports, Valentia Harbor in Ireland and Trinity Bay in Newfoundland, on August 5, 1858. Unfortunately, the engineer in charge used very high voltages that damaged the cable when messages were sent. It stopped working within a few weeks.

Great Eastern

Several years later another attempt was made. The biggest ship of the time, the Great Eastern, was used to carry all the cable. In 1865 she laid 1,200 miles of cable before it broke. The ship tried again. On July 27, 1866 the cable was pulled ashore in Newfoundland. Immediately the Great Eastern returned to the point where the first cable had broken. Crew members found the end, spliced it, and completed laying a second cable. From then on undersea telegraph cables increased rapidly, linking all parts of the world.

Guglielmo Marconi is shown here with his assistants George Kemp (left) and P.W. Paget (right). They are shown at Signal Hill in Newfoundland shortly before receiving the first wireless signals sent across the Atlantic Ocean. Scientists were so certain that electromagnetic waves could not travel that far that at first they did not believe that Marconi had succeeded.

4

All the Ships at Sea

The next few years were filled with constant activity. In March 1897, Marconi used balloons and kites to get aerials into the air over Salisbury Plain. There he transmitted signals for more than four miles. Two months later he made a successful transmission across the Bristol Channel, a distance of over eight and a half miles. It was the first signal sent across water.

The news of Marconi's invention spread rapidly. Those who had anything to do with ships realized immediately how important wireless could be for ship-to-shore communication and for communication between ships. The telegraph wires that sent messages across great distances on land—and even between continents by undersea cables— were of no use to ships. They couldn't cross the oceans dragging wires behind them.

They desperately needed something. As author Gavin Weightman notes, "If they hit an iceberg, a common hazard in the North Atlantic in spring, or their engines failed, or they caught fire, they had no means of calling for assistance. . . . Every year passenger and cargo ships disappeared, many leaving no survivors or clues to the fate that had befallen them."[1]

The Italian Navy realized how important Marconi's wireless signals were. They were surprised to find one of their own citizens making such progress in England. As an Italian citizen, Marconi was required to serve in the Italian military. But he did not want to leave England. He wanted to continue his experiments with support and financing from the post office. He also wanted to form a private company to profit from his invention.

His relatives in England thought he should become a British citizen. He spoke English fluently. In fact, his English was still better than his Italian. But Guglielmo loved Italy. He didn't know what to do, so he talked to the Italian Ambassador about his problem. The ambassador came up with a solution that pleased everyone. Guglielmo was inducted into the Italian Navy and assigned to the London Embassy. His duties were to continue his experiments.

Soon he was invited to Italy to demonstrate his invention to the King and Queen of Italy. He continued experimenting at the dockyard in Spezia where he made an important discovery. Signals could be sent and received when a ship had traveled out of sight below the horizon. This could only mean that the electromagnetic waves somehow followed the curvature of the earth.

While Marconi was in Italy, his supporters in England founded The Wireless Telegraph and Signal Company. Soon it would become known as the Marconi Wireless and Signal Company. Marconi was given 15,000 English pounds ($750,000 in today's money) and 60,000 of the shares in the company in exchange for his patents. He also received the equivalent of more than $1,000,000 to conduct further research. In only three years from the time he began experimenting in the attic at Villa Griffone, he had become both famous and rich.

Marconi's company set up wireless stations in England to continue experiments. Marconi himself worked on ships at sea to develop communications between ships and shore. He made rapid progress and the year 1898 became especially fruitful. The wireless, as it had become known, was used twice to save lives and cargo in shipping accidents off the mouth of the Thames River. His company got a contract to supply

Men assembling wireless compo-
nents at the Marconi Wireless
Telegraph Works in Chelmsford,
Essex, England.

Factory workers making insulating
cones at the Marconi Wireless
Telegraph Works in England.

information about the movement of ships for the insurance company
Lloyds of London.

Then as now, the public was more interested in sports than in
insurance statistics. Marconi broadcast reports of the Kingstown yacht
races, transmitting from a tugboat to the Dublin *Daily Express* as the
race was in progress.

By now nearly everyone in England knew of Marconi's work. Queen
Victoria wanted to set up communications between her summer home
and her son, the Prince of Wales. He was on a yacht that was anchored
several miles offshore. She sent a request to Marconi, asking him to
establish a wireless connection. While Marconi was in the royal gardens
setting up the aerial, he was ordered to leave because the queen would
be using the area. The young inventor abruptly returned to his hotel.
Queen Victoria said, "Get another electrician!" They told her, "Alas, your
Majesty, England has no Marconi."[2] The Queen sent a carriage to his
hotel. She met him and thanked him for setting up the transmission,
which she used dozens of times.

The incident with Queen Victoria reveals much about Marconi's
character. He impressed people with his faultlessly correct manners and
courtesy. He was polite to everyone but feared no one. He did not feel
inferior to famous scientists (many of whom told him his plans were

impossible), ambassadors, high-ranking officers, or kings and queens. He had one aim, and one only: to send his wireless signals farther and farther and farther.

He took another step in that direction in the spring of 1899 with the first international transmission. He sent a message 31 miles from England to France across the English Channel. In July, Marconi wireless was installed on three British warships that were able to communicate with each other over distances of 60 miles.

Despite these successes, the other directors of his company were shocked when he told them he intended to build two new stations that were more powerful than any that had been built before. He intended to send messages across the Atlantic Ocean.

The site Marconi selected in England was on the far southwest coast at Poldhu in Cornwall. After a storm destroyed a station attempted on Cape Cod, Massachusetts, Marconi established the North American station at St. John's, Newfoundland, an island at the easternmost tip of Canada. Several attempts at transmission from Poldhu to St. John's were made. Storms wrecked the antennas. Balloons and kites sent up in the gale force winds were torn loose.

Finally, on December 12, 1901, shortly after noon, Marconi heard three clicks on the telephone attached to the receiver. His assistant Kemp also heard the signal, Morse code for the letter S. They heard it again. And once more. Then bad weather closed in again, blowing away the balloons that supported the antennas. When Marconi reported his success at sending a transmission across the Atlantic, almost no one believed him.

Scientists still insisted that it was impossible to send wireless signals that far. They said that Marconi had only heard atmospheric static from the storms, not signals from England. The curve of the earth meant that there was an enormous mountain of water between the transmitter and the receiver. And electromagnetic waves could travel only in a straight line. Therefore it was impossible for the signals to travel across the ocean.

Marconi didn't agree. He didn't know why, but he knew that in Italy he had sent signals to ships that had sailed over the horizon. Therefore, he reasoned, the problem was not the curve of the earth. The problem was creating a signal strong enough to travel thousands of miles. What neither Marconi nor the scientists knew then was that the earth's surface reflected the waves. The waves then traveled up to the ionosphere, an atmospheric layer high above the earth. The ionosphere reflected the waves back to the earth's surface, which again reflected them to the ionosphere. And so the electromagnetic waves crossed the ocean, not in a straight line, but back and forth like a ball bouncing between two parallel walls.

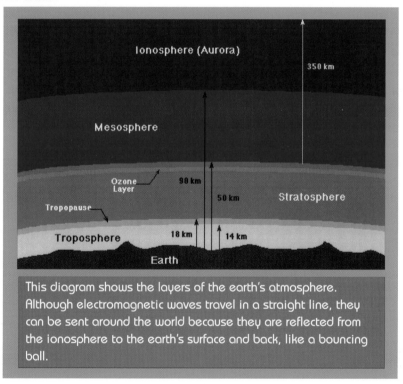

Ionosphere (Aurora)

350 km

Mesosphere

Ozone Layer   90 km

50 km   Stratosphere

Tropopause

Troposphere   18 km   14 km

Earth

This diagram shows the layers of the earth's atmosphere. Although electromagnetic waves travel in a straight line, they can be sent around the world because they are reflected from the ionosphere to the earth's surface and back, like a bouncing ball.

Back in England two months later, Marconi silenced all doubts by building a very high aerial on a ship traveling west. It received messages from the station at Poldhu at a range of 1,550 miles. Making many trips back and forth across the Atlantic in the following years, Marconi and his assistants developed the radio system for public use.

An interruption in Marconi's steady devotion to his work occurred in 1904 when he fell in love with Beatrice O'Brien, a young Irish woman (as his mother had been). They were married the following year. Their first daughter died in infancy, but they had three more children: a daughter, Degna, born in 1908; a son, Giulio, born in 1910; and another daughter, Gioia, born in 1916.

His efforts eventually brought him the highest honor the scientific world has to offer. In 1909, he shared the Nobel Prize in physics with Karl Ferdinand Braun.

The importance of his work had been dramatically demonstrated earlier that year. In January, two passenger liners—the *Republic* and the *Florida*—collided soon after the *Republic* had left New York. Even though the *Republic's* electrical system was destroyed, the wireless remained undamaged. The operator switched to emergency batteries and sent a call for help. A radio station on Nantucket Island received the signal and transmitted it to nearby ships. They quickly came to the *Republic's* aid and rescued hundreds of passengers and crewmen. It marked the first use of emergency radio on the high seas.

The *Great Republic* was the largest merchant ship of its day. It was bound from Nova Scotia to London in 1872 when it began leaking and sank, unable to communicate about the disaster. Two years later Guglielmo Marconi was born, the man whose invention would make it possible for ships at sea to send messages.

An even more dramatic example of the importance of Marconi's wireless system occurred in the most famous disaster at sea, the sinking of the *Titanic* in 1912. Marconi and his wife had planned to travel on the *Titanic*. He changed his travel plans because of business pressures. Beatrice canceled hers at the last minute because her two-year-old son was sick. Those who survived the *Titanic* disaster gave thanks to Marconi. Without wireless, many of them could have died before being rescued because no one would have known where they were.

A little past noon on April 10, 1912, the luxury liner Titanic left Southampton, England, on her first voyage across the Atlantic Ocean. The event was widely reported in the newspapers because the Titanic was the largest and most luxurious passenger liner ever built. Furthermore, the ship was believed to be unsinkable. Many wealthy and famous people had booked passage on the Titanic.

Titanic

A little before midnight on April 14, the ship struck an iceberg and sank within three hours. Of more than 2,200 passengers and crewmembers aboard the Titanic, only 705 were saved. The rest died in the icy North Atlantic waters. The closest ship to the Titanic was the Californian, on its way from London to Boston. The Californian's captain had decided to stop for the night rather than continue through the ice field. He asked his wireless operator to send a message about the ice to the Titanic. The Titanic's wireless operator responded, telling the Californian operator to shut up. He was busy with messages that passengers had asked him to send. Soon he was sending a different type of message, desperately begging for help as the water began creeping over the Titanic's deck.

Carpathia

The operator on the Californian had been working for two shifts. After hearing the Titanic's earlier reply he shut off his radio and went to his quarters to sleep. He was the only operator on board. If the radio on the Californian had not been turned off or the ship had carried two wireless operators, many more people might have been saved. The Californian was less than 20 miles from the Titanic. The liner Carpathia was 58 miles away when it received the distress signal from the Titanic. The Carpathia immediately headed for the sinking ship at full speed, reaching the survivors in four hours.

This tragedy has fascinated people for nearly 100 years. It dramatically demonstrated the importance of radio communications at sea.

After achieving fame and wealth for his invention of wireless telegraphy, Guglielmo Marconi purchased a luxurious yacht, the *Elettra*, in 1919. The yacht was outfitted as a floating laboratory as well as a place to entertain his wealthy friends. He is shown here in the radio room of the yacht, where he continued his experiments in short-wave transmissions.

5

Businessman and Politician

Guglielmo's success in transmitting wireless signals over long distances both increased his business opportunities and increased the problems facing his company. The telegraph companies that had spent fortunes laying the transatlantic cables were upset when Marconi succeeded in sending messages. They brought lawsuits trying to stop the use of wireless signals. They failed, but the legal battles took time and money.

In 1913, Marconi's company was involved in a scandal. Some opponents claimed the contract between the British government and Marconi for an Imperial Wireless Scheme had been awarded through bribery. Government ministers were accused of using confidential information to profit by purchasing stock in the company. In the investigations into what was called "the Marconi Scandal," no evidence of bribery was found. Marconi was never personally accused of any wrongdoing. He was bitter at having his name attached to the scandal.

Plans for the Imperial Wireless Scheme, a system to join all of the British Empire by wireless, were abandoned the following year when World War I started. When Italy joined the Allies in 1915, Marconi immediately offered his services to the Italian military. His main technical contribution during the war was a system of shortwave communications. He also developed a system that was able to detect the source of enemy signals.

When the United States entered the war in 1917, he went to America as an unofficial ambassador. After the war ended in 1918, he made two official visits to England. His loyalty to Italy and his command of English made him an excellent diplomat. Marconi went to the Paris Peace Conference in 1919. He was disappointed at the conference because Italy's war efforts were not recognized as much as he thought they should be.

In 1920, he was able to return to his scientific research. The previous year he bought a yacht, the *Elettra*. The name means "electricity" in Italian. He outfitted the yacht as a floating laboratory where he could conduct his experiments in short-wave transmissions. He was also able to entertain his wealthy and powerful friends. His wife grew tired of their many separations and the other women he entertained, and divorced him in 1923.

Meanwhile the British government was slow in pursuing the Imperial Wireless Scheme that had been abandoned at the beginning of the war. In 1924 Marconi proposed an entirely different project based on short-wave stations, which only the Marconi Company would be able to operate. The British accepted.

Marconi's hard work paid off when the first transmissions were sent between England and Canada in 1926. Stations were then built in South Africa, India, Australia, and South America. The worldwide communication network he had dreamed of was a reality at last.

Marconi married a second time in 1927, this time to a Roman aristocrat, Cristina Bezzi-Scali. Their active social life, and their daughter Elettra (who was born in 1930), took up most of Marconi's failing energies. He took a far less active part in the Marconi Company.

He did continue his experiments, however. He had become interested in shortwave radiation and its use in detecting the presence of ships and aircraft. In 1933 he had noticed that a car passing a mile

Guglielmo Marconi is shown here with his second wife, the wealthy Roman society woman Cristina Bezzi-Scali. With them is the only child of this second marriage, daughter Maria Elettra Elena Anna.

away was causing interference on his radio. He figured out that the radio waves had bounced off the car. That led him to experiment secretly for the Italian government. These experiments resulted in the development of radar (radio detection and ranging), a system of detecting objects at a distance by bouncing radio waves off of them.

At a lecture in New York he said, "It seems to me that it should be possible to design apparatus by means of which a ship could radiate or project a divergent beam of these rays in any desired direction, which rays, in coming across a metallic object such as another steamer or ship, would be reflected back to a receiver."[1] As usual, once he envisioned a possibility, he worked tirelessly to achieve it.

In his last years, Marconi also became interested in microwaves. Noting their heat-producing nature, he developed a therapy that is still called Marconi therapy. This technique is used to soothe pain in joints and muscles. He also undertook various diplomatic missions for the Italian government. He was loyal to the Fascist dictator, Benito Mussolini.

After suffering several heart attacks, Guglielmo Marconi died in Rome on July 20, 1937. News of his death spread rapidly around the world, thanks to his own development of a communication system that covered the entire earth. Radio stations everywhere observed two minutes of silence to honor his passing.

It was an appropriate tribute. The technology of our world could not exist without the use of the many types of electromagnetic waves. Marconi's tireless experiments revealed many of the amazing properties of these waves. His discoveries were the foundation upon which many other scientific developments of the 20th century were built.

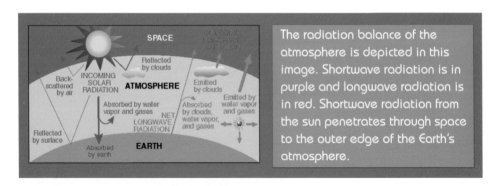

The radiation balance of the atmosphere is depicted in this image. Shortwave radiation is in purple and longwave radiation is in red. Shortwave radiation from the sun penetrates through space to the outer edge of the Earth's atmosphere.

The electromagnetic waves that Marconi worked with vary greatly in length—the distance between the crest of one wave and the crest of the next. The longest radio waves can be 12 miles in length. Two other ways of measuring radio waves are by their amplitude (or height), and their frequency. AM (amplitude modulation) radio stations vary the height of the waves they send out, while FM (frequency modulation) stations vary the frequency of the waves. This means that many radio stations can broadcast at the same time because they are using different types and different lengths of waves. When we tune in to a radio station, we alter the receiver to pick up a particular wave. There are over 10,000 radio stations—both AM and FM—operating in the United States.

Television began to replace radio as the primary entertainment medium in the 1950s and 1960s. Television broadcasts use radio waves that are between three and 20 feet long. These waves can carry both visual and sound images. Radar uses waves that range from half an inch to 40 inches in length. Cellular phones operate on wavelengths of about 12 to 16 inches.

The microwave ovens that we use to rapidly thaw and heat food use waves that are five inches or less in length. These same waves are also used in radio communication systems in space, and between the earth and satellites. Now we have powerful microwave receivers—like enormous ears—listening for radio waves from distant galaxies.

All these devices demonstrate the truth of the conclusion of Giancarlo Masini's excellent biography of Marconi. Masini says, "His first concern was what his experiments would mean for others, whether it was for saving lives at sea or advancing mutual understanding among the people of the world. It is almost impossible to conceive of life today without Marconi's extraordinary contributions."[2]

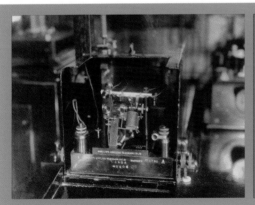

Marconi's wireless telegraph was used on the *Carpathia*, the ship which received the distress call from the sinking *Titanic* and traveled the 58 miles between them in four hours to rescue the survivors. Another ship, the *Californian*, was less than 20 miles from the *Titanic*, but its wireless receiver was turned off.

Karl Jansky

In 1928, Karl Jansky went to work for the Bell Telephone Laboratories. The company assigned him to investigate sources of static that could interfere with radio voice transmissions. He built an antenna mounted on a turntable so it could turn in any direction. It became known as "Jansky's merry-go-round."

After several months he had found static that came from thunderstorms and another kind of static that he couldn't identify. It got stronger once a day. At first he thought it was radiation from the sun. But it wasn't. He finally figured out that the radiation came from the center of the Milky Way galaxy.

Scientists were very excited by Jansky's discovery. He wanted Bell Labs to build a 100-foot diameter dish antenna for more studies, but they refused. Not until after World War II did universities and foundations begin to build the large radio telescopes needed to gather more signals from space.

VLBA

In June of 2003, scientists from around the world gathered in Socorro, New Mexico, to celebrate the 10th anniversary of a radio telescope that is wider than the continent. It is called the Very Long Baseline Array (VLBA). It includes ten 240-ton radio-telescope antennas that are located from Hawaii to the Virgin Islands and are operated from Socorro.

The VLBA is like a huge eye 5,000 miles wide. It can produce the sharpest images of any telescope on earth or in space. Since it was established in 1993, the VLBA has measured the distance of objects beyond the Milky Way galaxy. It has mapped the magnetic fields of stars and charted distant supernova explosions.

The VLBA can also produce very exact measurements on earth. Scientists use it to record movement of the earth's tectonic plates, irregularities in the planet's rotation, and changes in climate. Many scientists hope that the VLBA will help them discover intelligent life in other places in the universe. Maybe some Marconi in another galaxy is sending us signals.

Chronology

1874	Born on April 25 in Bologna, Italy
1877	Travels to England with his mother
1880	Returns to Italy
1887	Fails admission examination for Leghorn Naval Academy; enrolls in Leghorn Technical Institute to study physics and chemistry
1894	Fails entrance examinations for University of Bologna; begins experiments with wireless signals
1895	Sends signal over hill near Villa Griffone; attempts to interest Italian Post Office in his invention
1896	Travels to England with his mother; meets Sir William Preece, Chief Engineer of the English Post Office and begins demonstrations of wireless
1897	Sends signals more than eight miles across Bristol Channel; sends first ship-to-shore signals for the Italian Navy; "Wireless Telegraph Company" founded in England
1898	Sets up wireless transmission system for Queen Victoria
1899	Sends first international signal across the English Channel to France
1901	Sends Morse code signal "S" from Poldhu, England across the Atlantic to Newfoundland, Canada
1905	Marries Beatrice O'Brien
1909	Awarded the Nobel Prize for Physics jointly with Karl Ferdinand Braun of Germany
1912	Loses an eye in an automobile accident
1915– 1918	Performs diplomatic missions for Italy during World War I
1919	Serves as Italian delegate to Paris Peace Conference; buys yacht *Elettra*
1923	Divorces Beatrice; joins Fascist party
1927	Marries Christina Bezzi-Scali
1937	Dies of heart failure on July 20 in Rome at the age of 63; radio stations all over the world observe two minutes of silence to honor him

Timeline of Discovery

1800	Alessandro Volta invents the electric battery.
1819	Danish scientist Hans Christian Oersted discovers that electricity and magnetism are closely related.
1825	William Sturgeon develops the first electromagnet.
1844	Samuel Morse sends the first telegraph message; it travels from Washington, D.C., to Baltimore.
1859	Gaston Plante invents the rechargeable battery.
1861	The transcontinental telegraph line connects New York and San Francisco.
1866	The transatlantic telegraph cable is successfully laid.
1873	James Clerk-Maxwell develops the theory of electromagnetic waves.
1887	Heinrich Hertz devises an experiment to prove Clerk-Maxwell's theory.
1897	Alexander Popov in Russia transmits radio waves over a distance of three miles.
1904	John Fleming invents the thermionic two-electrode valve, which makes it possible to transmit sound.
1906	Reginald Fessenden transmits the human voice.
1909	The *Republic* sends the first distress signal from a ship after colliding with the *Florida*.
1932	Karl Jansky discovers a strong source of radio static originating from center of our galaxy, the Milky Way.
1934	The Federal Communications Commission (FCC) is formed to regulate transmission and reception, grant licenses, and distribute frequencies for radio stations
1938	There are 650 transmitters and 26 million receivers in the United States.
1942	Radio emissions from the sun are detected for the first time.
1944	BBC broadcasts coded messages to resistance fighters in France announcing the Allied landings.
1957	The U.S.S.R. launches *Sputnik 1*, the first artificial satellite; it transmits radio signals back to earth.
1961	The FCC authorizes FM stereo broadcasting.
1962	The United States launches the Telstar satellite, which transmits video images across the Atlantic Ocean.
1972	Landsat 1, the first "eye-in-the-sky" satellite, is launched.
1974	Antony Hewish and Martin Ryle win the Nobel Prize in physics for discovering radio pulsars.
1978	Arno Penzias and Robert Wilson win the Nobel Prize in physics for the discovery of cosmic background radiation that supports the Big Bang theory of the creation of the universe.
1983	The first commercial cell phone network in the United States begins service.
1985	U.S. television networks begin satellite distribution to their affiliates.
1997	Mars Pathfinder transmits more than 17,000 images to earth after its successful landing.
2003	Scientists celebrate 10 years of successful operation of the Very Long Baseline Array in Socorro, New Mexico.
2004	Radio Waves, a Smiths Group Company, announces 23 GHz discriminator (TM) antenna providing Category A performance in low-profile package.

Chapter Notes

Chapter 1   The Dinner Plates
    1. Degna Marconi, *My Father, Marconi* (New York: McGraw Hill, 1962), p. 23.
    2. Ibid., pp. 25–26.

Chapter 2   Moving Around
    1. Giancarlo Masini, *Marconi* (New York: Marsilio Publishers, 1976), p. 26.
    2. Marconi, Degna, *My Father, Marconi* (New York: McGraw Hill, 1962), p. 16.
    3.
    4. Masini, p. 33.
    5. Marconi, p. 18.
    6. W. P. Jolly, *Marconi* (New York: Stein and Day Publishers, 1972), p. 17.
    7. Masini, p. 46.

Chapter 3   Farther and Farther
    1. Giancarlo Masini, *Marconi* (New York: Marsilio Publishers, 1976), p. 59.
    2. Ibid, p. 61.
    3. Ibid., p. 91.

Chapter 4   All the Ships at Sea
    1. Gavin Weightman, *Signor Marconi's Magic Box* (Cambridge, MA: Da Capo Press, 2003), p. 65.
    2. Degna Marconi, *My Father, Marconi* (New York: McGraw Hill, 1962), p. 66.

Chapter 5   Businessman and Politician
    1. Giancarlo Masini, *Marconi* (New York: Marsilio Publishers, 1976), p. 292.
    2. Ibid., p. 366.

Glossary

aerial (AIR-ee-ul)—a device for converting electrical waves to electrical current.

amplitude (AM-pluh-tood)—the height of electromagnetic waves.

battery (BAT-ur-ee)—two or more cells containing chemicals that produce a flow of electricity when they are linked together.

cable (KAY-bul)—an insulated conducting wire.

coherer (co-HAYR-ur)—electrical device in which metal particles cling together and conduct electricity under the influence of electromagnetic waves.

conductor (kun-DUCK-tur)—material through which electricity flows easily.

electric current (ee-LEK-trik CUR-unt)—the flow of electricity through a substance such as a metal wire.

electromagnetic waves (ee-lek-tro-mag-NET-ik WAYVZ)—waves with features of both electricity and magnetism that can travel through air.

frequency (FREE-kwun-see)—the number of complete electromagnetic waves in one second.

ionosphere (eye-AWN-uhs-feer)—layer of ions high above the earth that reflects electromagnetic waves.

microwaves (MY-kro-wayvz)—electromagnetic waves with wavelengths between 12 inches and a fraction of an inch.

patent (PAT-unt)—legal document showing that someone is the official owner of rights to produce and use an invention.

receiver (ree-SEE-vur)—a device that detects radio waves and turns them into electrical signals.

shortwaves (SHORT-wayvz)—electromagnetic waves with wavelengths less than 100 yards.

telegraph (TELL-uh-graf)—system of sending messages in electrical currents through wires.

transmitter (tranz-MIT-ur)—a device that sends out radio waves.

wavelength (WAYV-length)—the distance from the highest point of one wave to the highest point of the next wave.

For Further Reading

For Young Adults

Birch, Beverley. *Guglielmo Marconi, Radio Pioneer.* Woodbridge, Connecticut: Blackbirch Press, 2001.

Goldsmith, Dr. Mike. *Guglielmo Marconi.* New York: Raintree Steck-Vaughn Publishers, 2003.

Parker, Steve. *Guglielmo Marconi and Radio.* Broomall, Pennsylvania: Chelsea House Publishers, 1995.

Tames, Richard. *Guglielmo Marconi.* New York: Franklin Watts, 1990.

Works Consulted

Jolly, W. P. *Marconi.* New York: Stein and Day Publishers, 1972.

Marconi, Degna. *My Father, Marconi.* New York: McGraw Hill, 1962.

Masini, Giancarlo. *Marconi.* New York: Marsilio Publishers, 1976.

Weightman, Gavin. *Signor Marconi's Magic Box.* Cambridge, Mass.: Da Capo Press, 2003.

On the Internet

Guglielmo Marconi—Biography for Nobel Prize in Physics
www.nobel.se/physics/laureates/1909/marconi-bio.html

Guglielmo Marconi—the complete photo guide for historians and collectors
www.etedeschi.ndirect.co.uk/marconi/

Guglielmo Marconi—The "father of Radio"
www.marconiusa.org/marconi/

Marconi Past and Present
www.marconicalling.com/introsting.htm

Marconi Foundation—Communication for Goodness Sake
http://www.marconifoundation.org/index_content.html

History Magazine—The Transatlantic Cable
http://www.history-magazine.com/cable.html

Electromagnetic Waves—different waves, different wavelengths
http://imagers.gsfc.nasa.gov/ems/waves3.html

Index